THIS BOOK

Belongs to

○ ○ ○ ○ ○ ○ ○ ○ ○ ○ ○ ○ ○ ○ ○ ○ ○ ○

Autumn season

Coloring Book

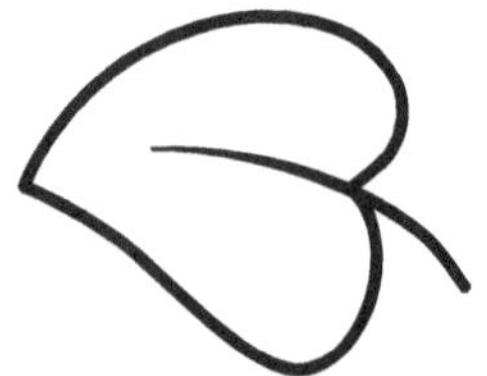

TEST YOUR COLORS HERE

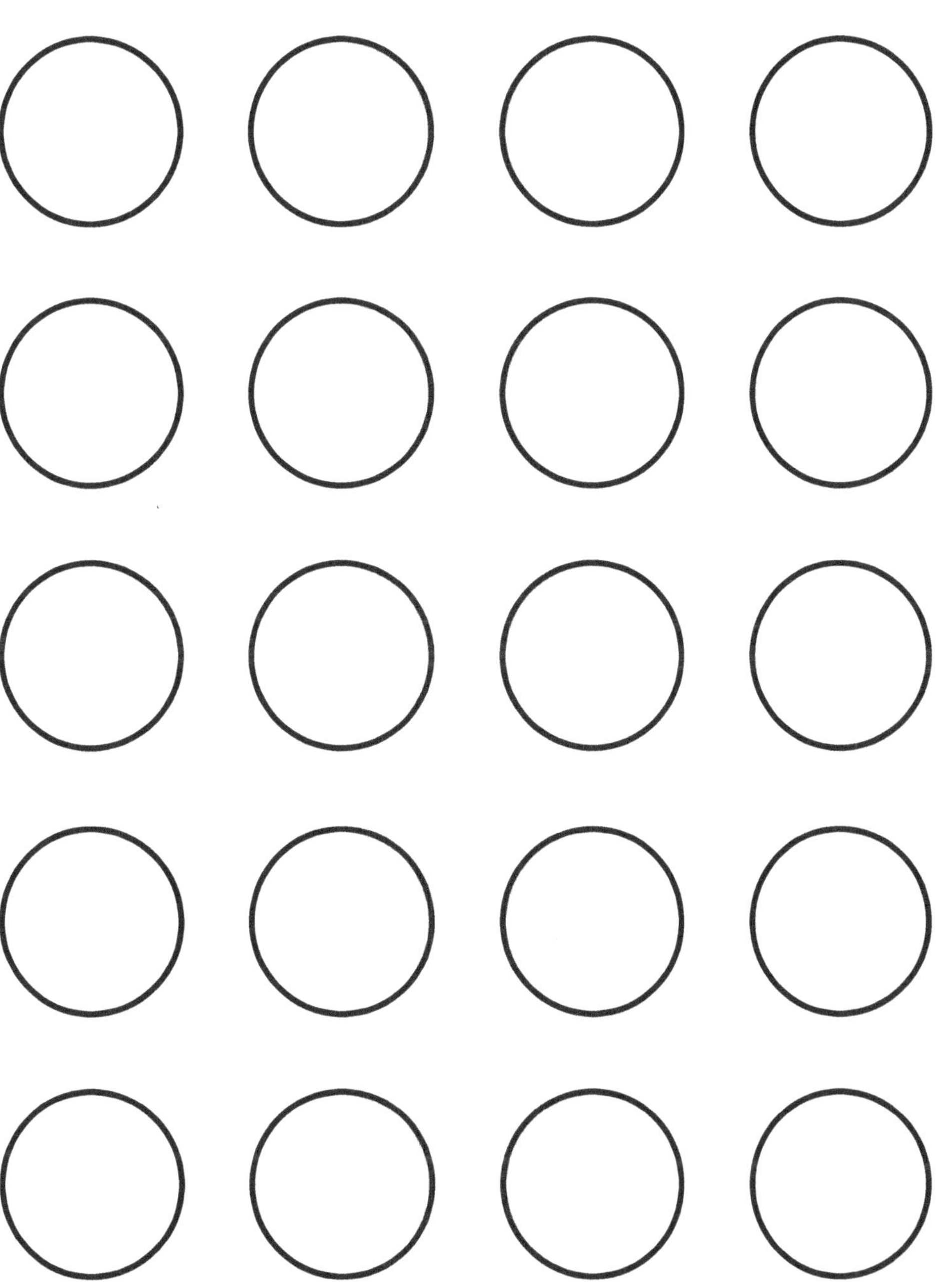

TRY TO REDRAW

TRY TO REDRAW

TRY TO REDRAW

TRY TO REDRAW

TRY TO REDRAW

TRY TO REDRAW

TRY TO REDRAW

TRY TO REDRAW

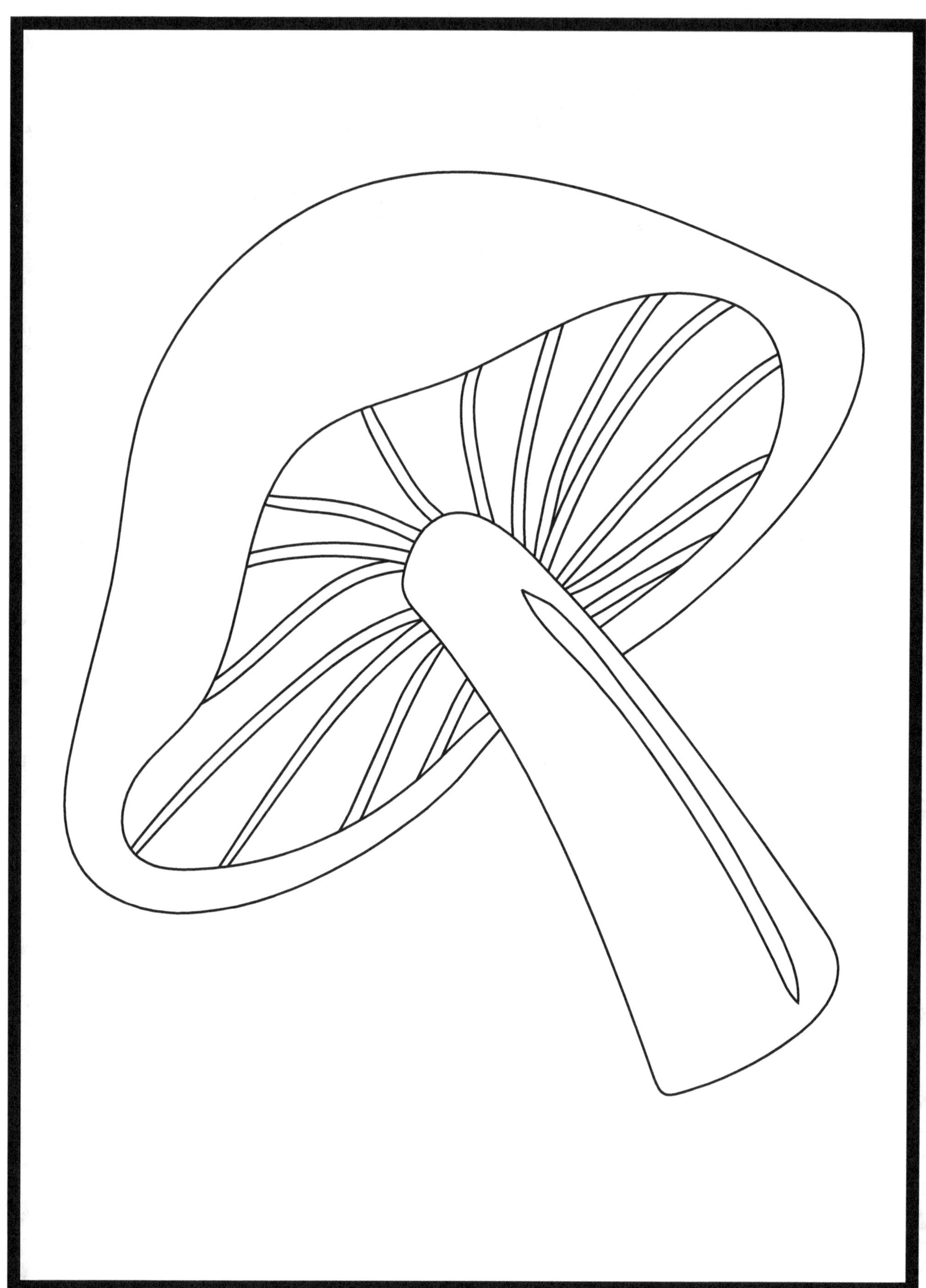

TRY TO REDRAW

TRY TO REDRAW

TRY TO REDRAW

TRY TO REDRAW

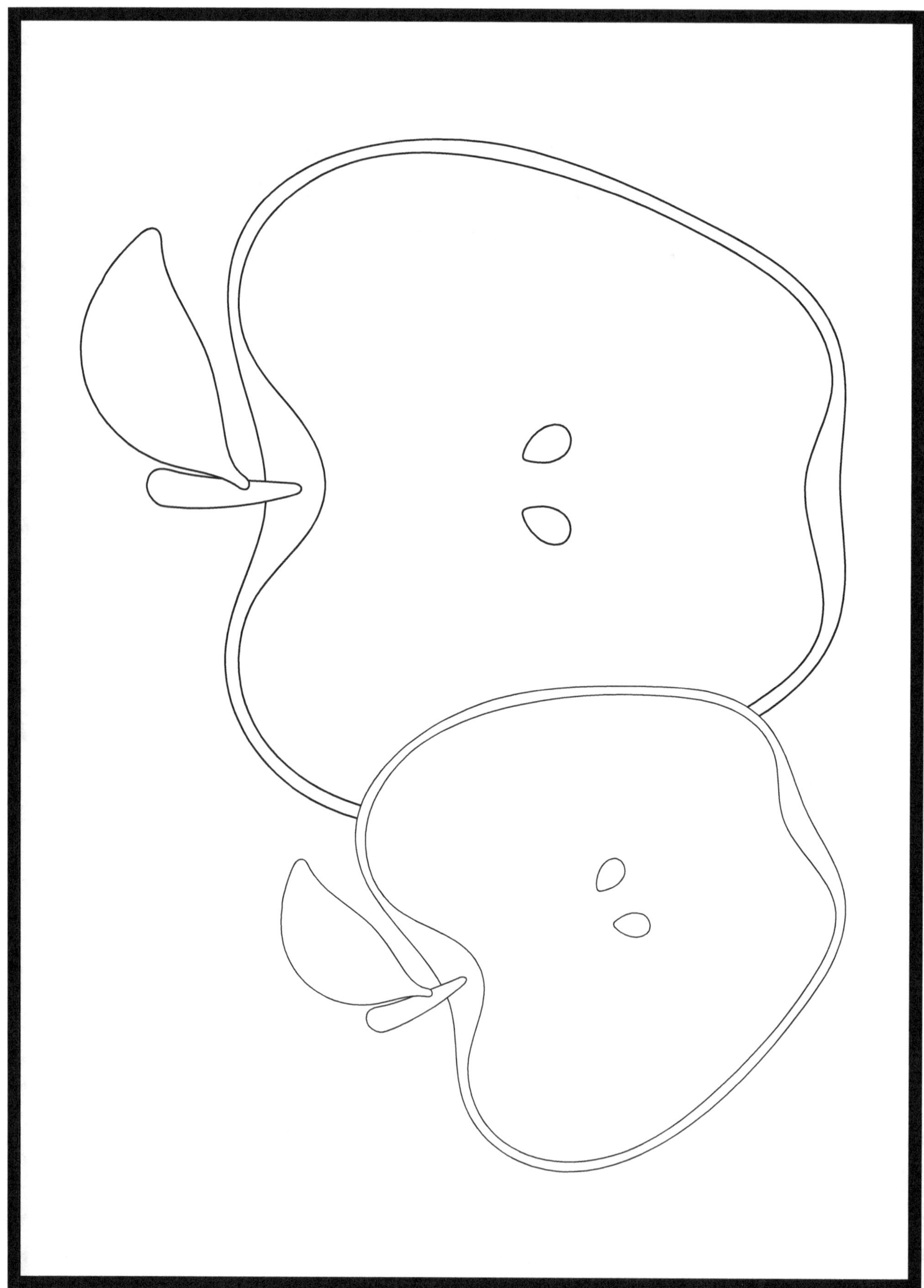

TRY TO REDRAW

TRY TO REDRAW

TRY TO REDRAW

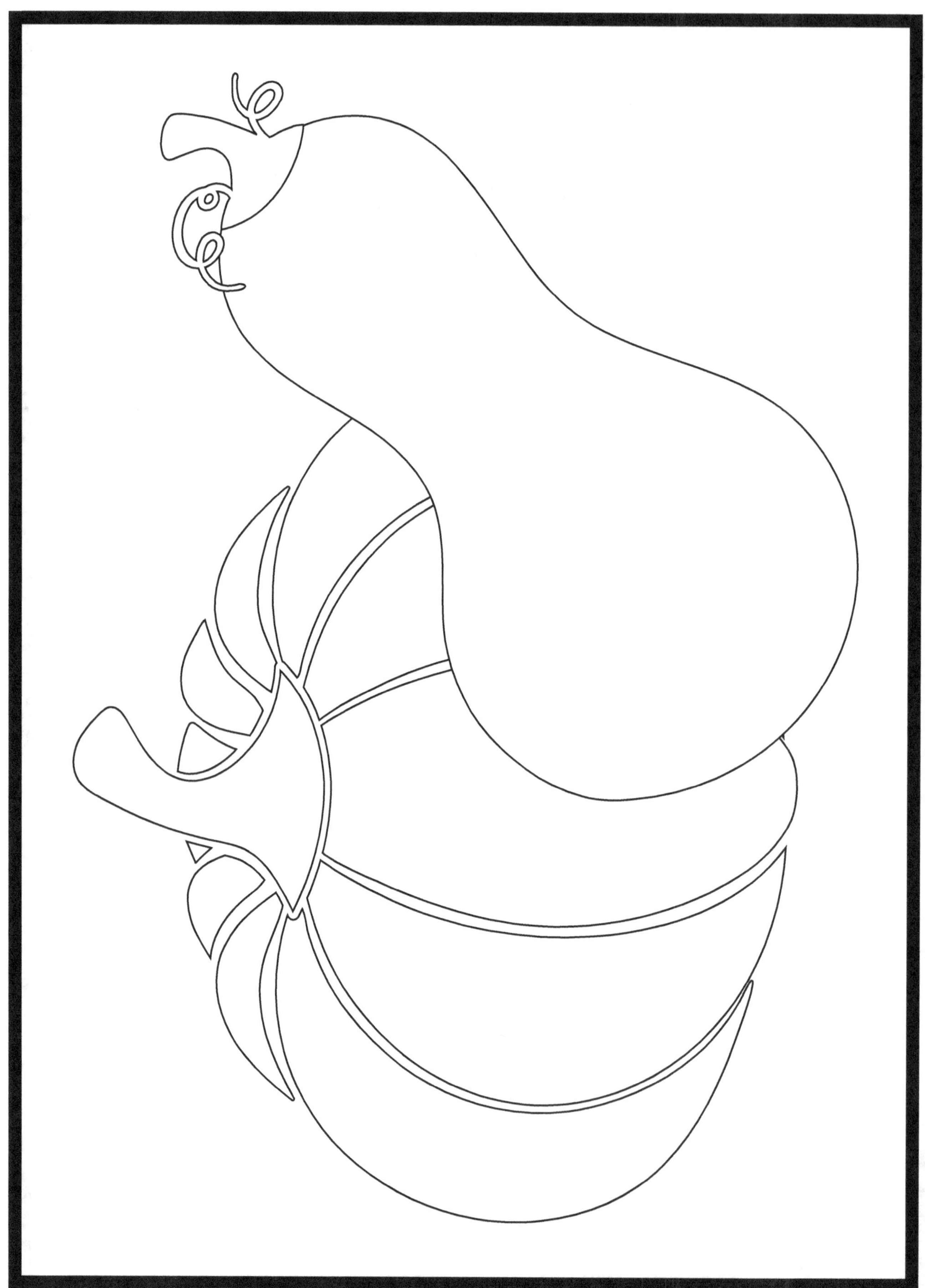

TRY TO REDRAW

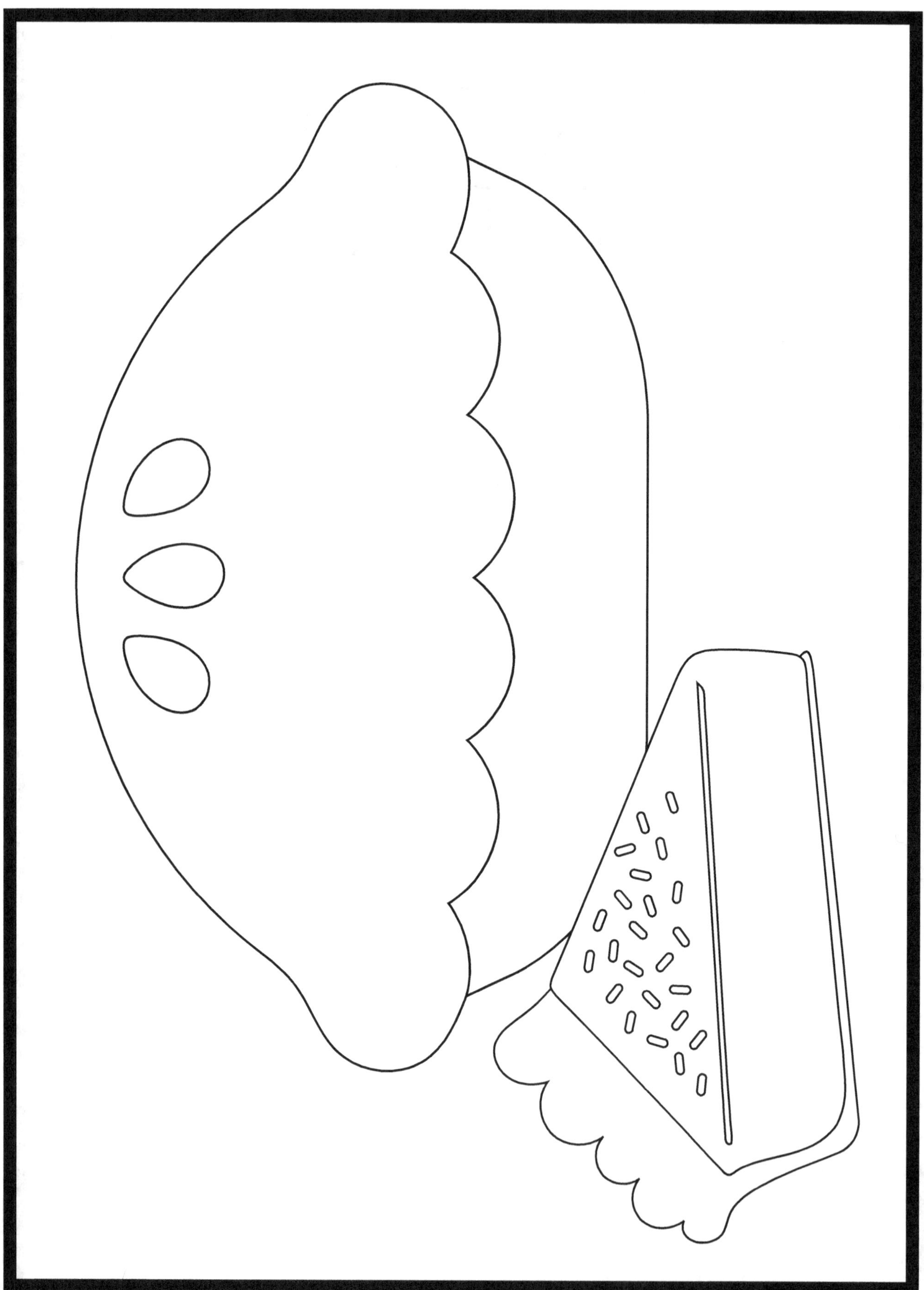

TRY TO REDRAW

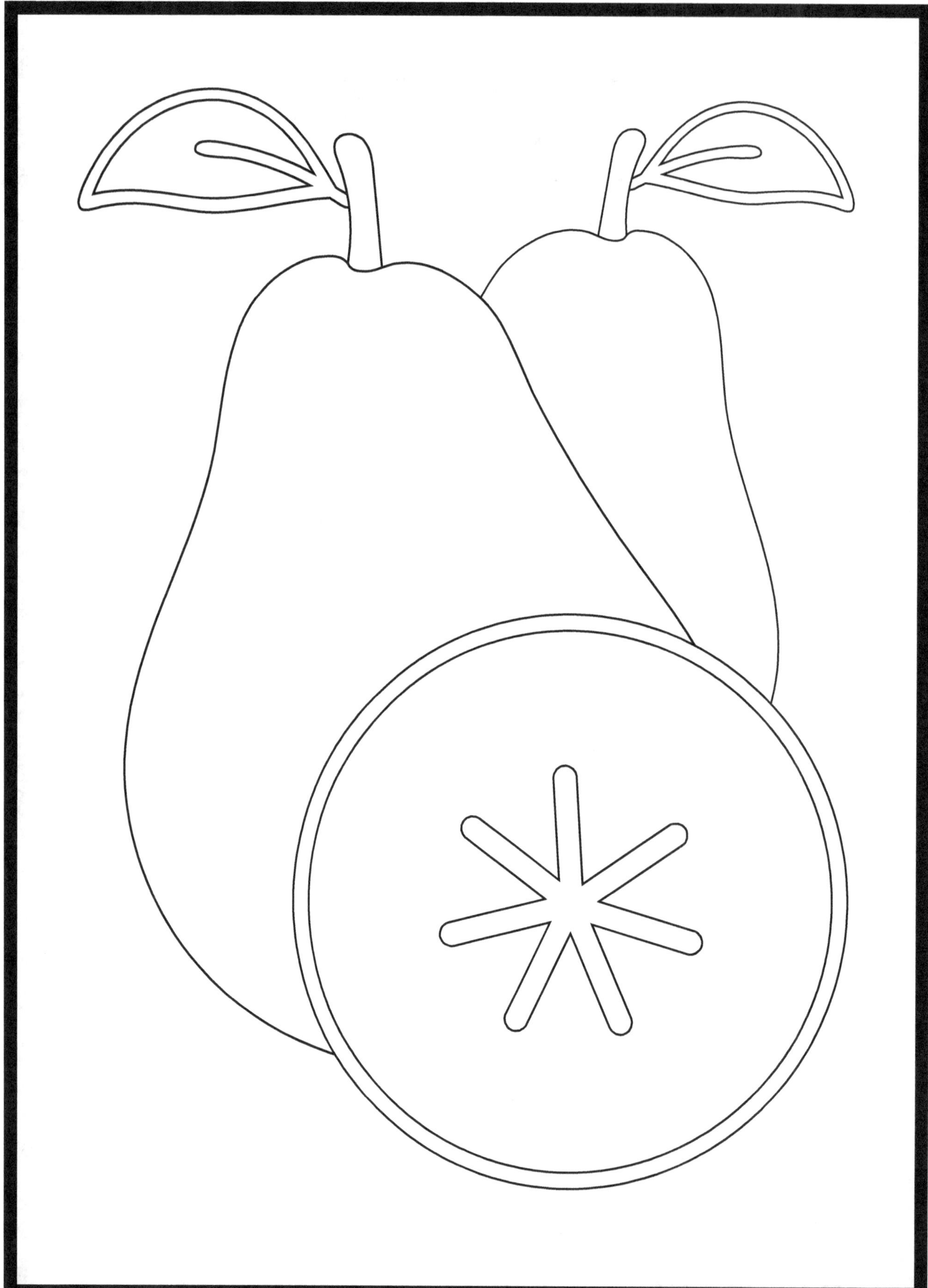

TRY TO REDRAW

The End